Rapping about Bodies of water

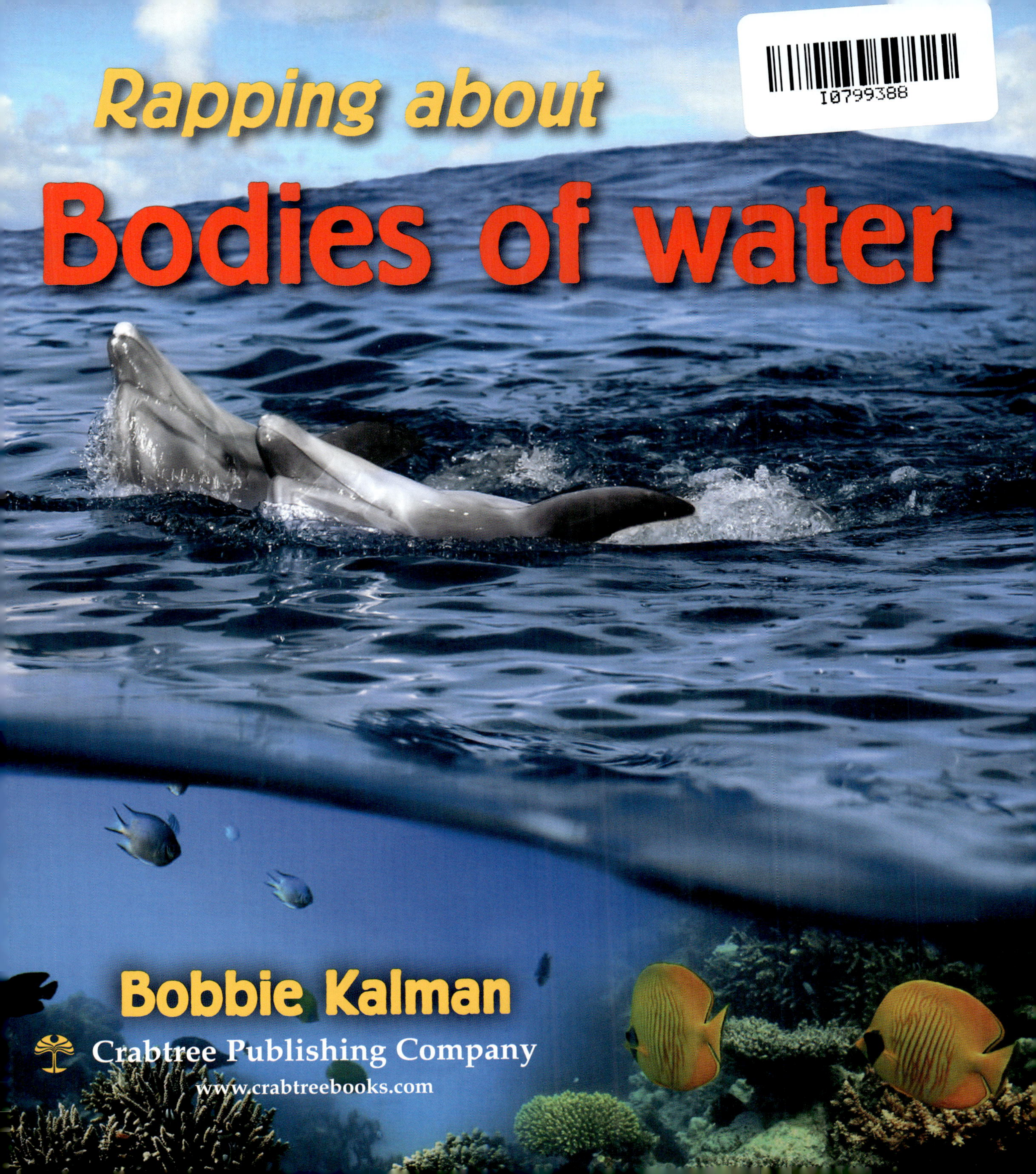

Bobbie Kalman

Crabtree Publishing Company
www.crabtreebooks.com

Created by Bobbie Kalman

For my husband Peter,
who loves to listen to rap with me
as we swim, sing, and dance
in the body of water in our back yard

Author and Editor-in-Chief
Bobbie Kalman

Editors
Kathy Middleton
Crystal Sikkens

Photo research
Bobbie Kalman

Design
Bobbie Kalman
Katherine Berti
Samantha Crabtree
(logo and front cover)

Print and production coordinator
Katherine Berti

Prepress technician
Katherine Berti

Illustrations
Barbara Bedell: pages 9 (all except yellow fish, purple fish, lionfish, and background), 12 (all except sea urchin)
Katherine Berti: pages 9 (yellow fish, purple fish, and background), 18–19
Cori Marvin: page 9 (lionfish)
Vanessa Parson-Robbs: page 12 (sea urchin)

Photographs
BigStockPhoto: page 17 (eggs)
iStockphoto: page 5 (bottom right)
river raft: Ron Hilton/Shutterstock: page 5 (bottom left)
Wikimedia: USDA/Ted Center: page 16 (right center); Dcrjsr: page 16 (right bottom)
All other images by Shutterstock

Library and Archives Canada Cataloguing in Publication

Kalman, Bobbie
Rapping about bodies of water / Bobbie Kalman.

(Rapping about--)
Includes index.
Issued also in electronic formats.
ISBN 978-0-7787-2795-8 (bound).--ISBN 978-0-7787-2802-3 (pbk.)

1. Bodies of water--Juvenile literature. 2. Water--Juvenile literature. I. Title. II. Series: Rapping about--

GB662.3.K337 2012 j553.7 C2012-900287-9

Library of Congress Cataloging-in-Publication Data

Kalman, Bobbie.
Rapping about bodies of water / Bobbie Kalman.
p. cm. -- (Rapping about)
Includes index.
ISBN 978-0-7787-2795-8 (reinforced library binding : alk. paper) -- ISBN 978-0-7787-2802-3 (pbk. : alk. paper) -- ISBN 978-1-4271-7910-4 (electronic pdf) -- ISBN 978-1-4271-8025-4 (electronic html)
1. Water--Juvenile literature. I. Title.

GB662.3.K3533 2012
551.46--dc23

2012000079

Crabtree Publishing Company
www.crabtreebooks.com 1-800-387-7650

Printed in the U.S.A./092015/CG20150812

Published in Canada
Crabtree Publishing
616 Welland Ave.
St. Catharines, Ontario
L2M 5V6

Published in the United States
Crabtree Publishing
PMB 59051
350 Fifth Avenue, 59th Floor
New York, New York 10118

Published in the United Kingdom
Crabtree Publishing
Maritime House
Basin Road North, Hove
BN41 1WR

Published in Australia
Crabtree Publishing
3 Charles Street
Coburg North
VIC 3058

Contents

Water on Earth

Earth is called the "blue planet."
Do you know why this is true?
Five huge **oceans** cover most of Earth,
so from space, our planet looks blue.
Look up! There is water in the clouds.
Look down! It is on the ground, too.
Did you know that water
is also in me and you?

ocean

What is a body of water?

A **body of water** is a place where water collects in a certain space. Bodies of water can be huge or small. They can be human-made or natural. These pictures show water. Have a good look! To learn more about water, read this fun book.

lake

river

pond

Earth's oceans

What is wet and salty and in constant motion?
It is a huge water body called an ocean.
Look at Earth's oceans on the map below.
How many are there? Do you know?
Can you name the oceans from large to small?
Were you able to name them all?

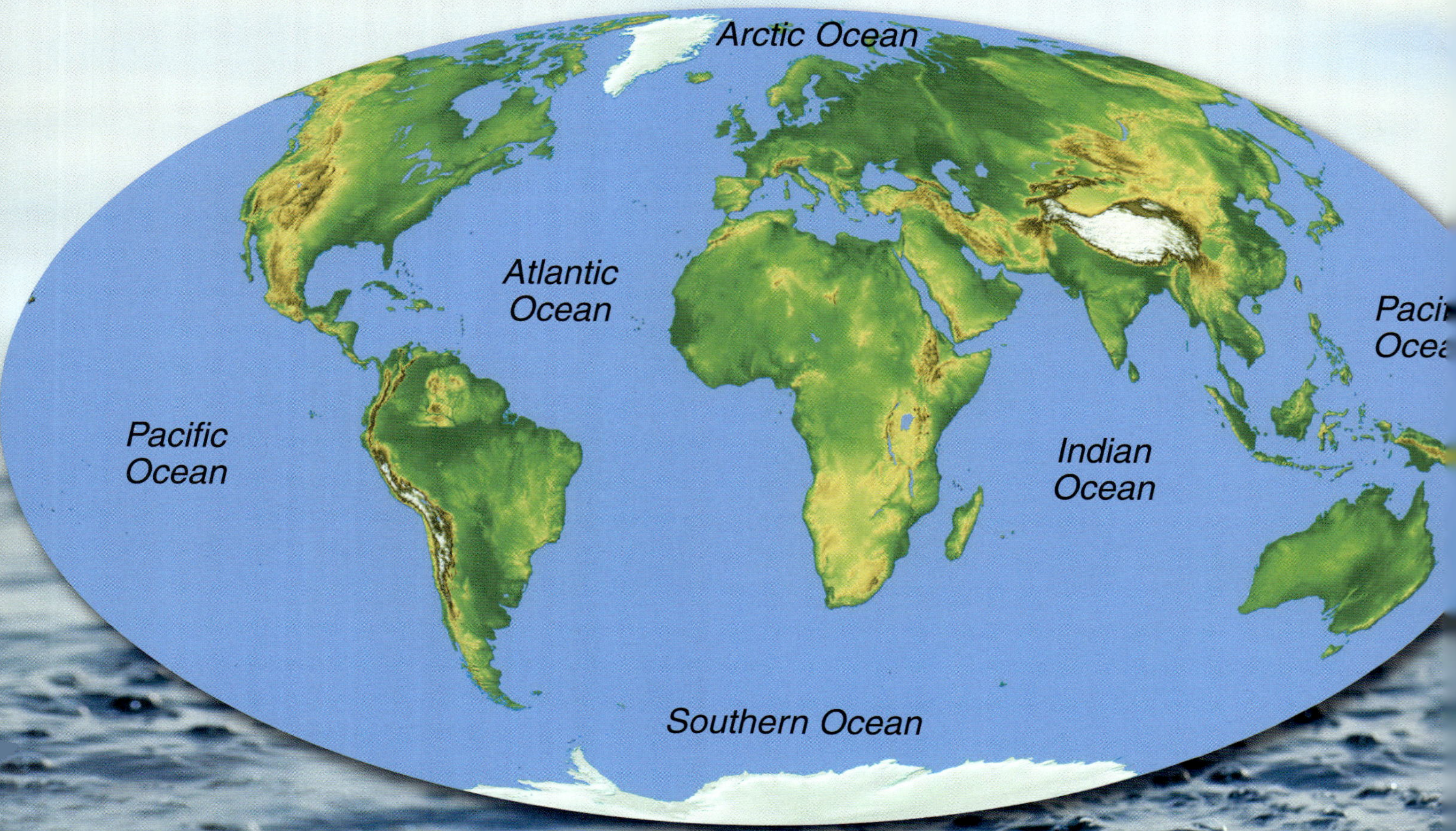

Which two oceans have a lot of ice?
Which ocean is so big
that its name appears twice?
An ocean near land
is often called a ***sea****.*
Name five seas that you can see.

Ocean water

Ocean water travels in **currents** and waves,
moving onto beaches and into sea caves.
The water can heat or cool the land.
The big waves it brings cover the sand.

*The **salt water** in oceans has a very strong taste.*
You can taste the salt when it splashes on your face.

Some parts of oceans are shallow and bright.
Others are deep and dark as the night.
Some ocean animals make their own light
in a **zone** of the ocean called **midnight**.

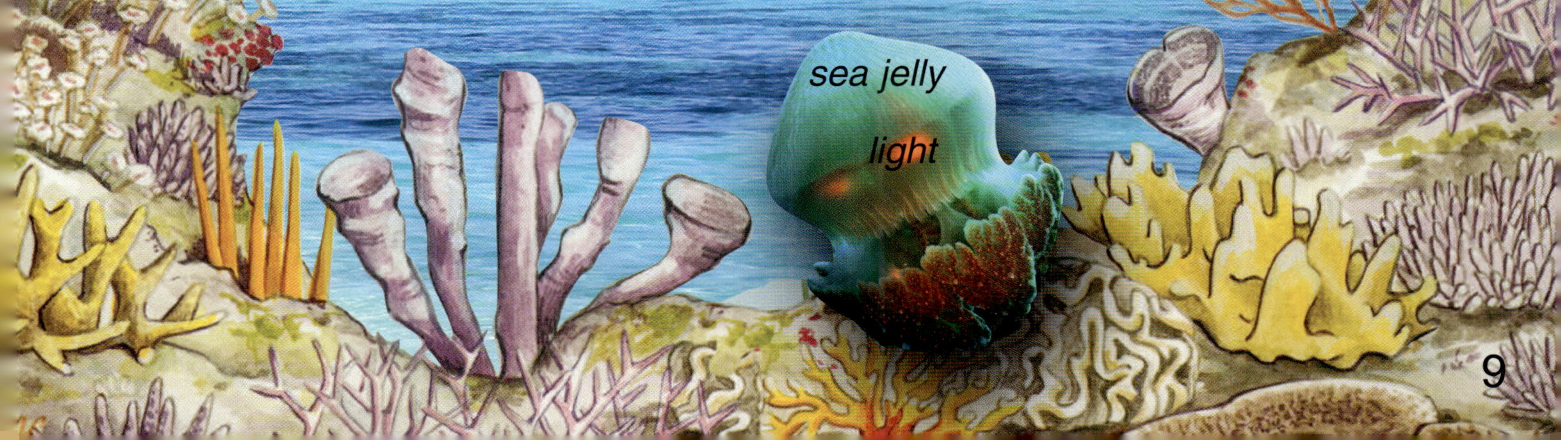

Water bodies at coasts

beach

Oceans touch land at many **coasts**. Coasts are the edges of land. Coasts can be covered in rocks or stones or have beaches of fine, soft sand. This group of coastline pictures explores the bodies of water at ocean shores.

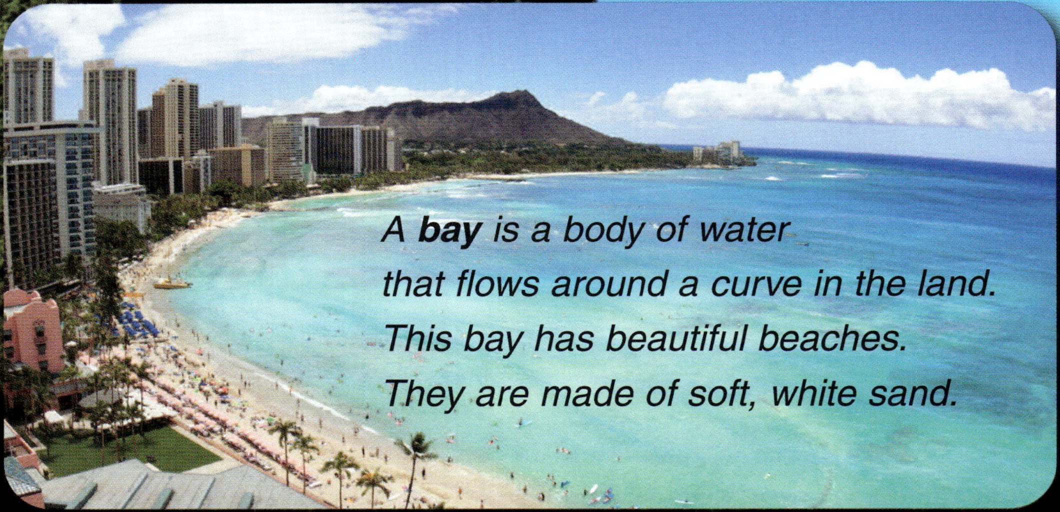

*A **bay** is a body of water that flows around a curve in the land. This bay has beautiful beaches. They are made of soft, white sand.*

A **harbor** is a **secluded** space
that keeps boats sheltered
and in their place.

The boy on the right is in a **lagoon**
separated from the ocean by land.
Its water is so calm and clear
that fish come to eat from his hand.

Nature's pools

Seashores have **tides**
that are high or low.
During **low tide**,
where does the water go?
When the ocean **recedes**,
or moves away from the shore,
it leaves **tide pools**
that are fun to explore.
Animals trapped between pockets of rocks
can stay alive when the water drops.
When the next **high tide** brings water onshore,
they are carried back to the ocean once more.
Not all the animals make it back.
Some end up as a seabird's snack.

These monkeys do not
mind a snowstorm.
They sit in a hot pool,
to keep themselves warm.
This **hot spring** is heated
under the ground.
The monkeys enjoy the
warm bath they have found.

Wetlands are lands
that are covered with water
for all or part of the year.
Animals that visit wetland pools,
are birds, alligators, and deer.

Deep lake waters

A **lake** is a large body of **fresh water** that is completely surrounded by land. The water in most lakes is still and deep, and its **shores** have rocks, stones, or sand. Some lakes are so big, they look like seas. In winter, parts of some lakes can freeze. Lakes provide much of the water we drink. Lake water may be in your tub or sink.

Lake Ontario is one of the Great Lakes. It is located in Canada and the United States.

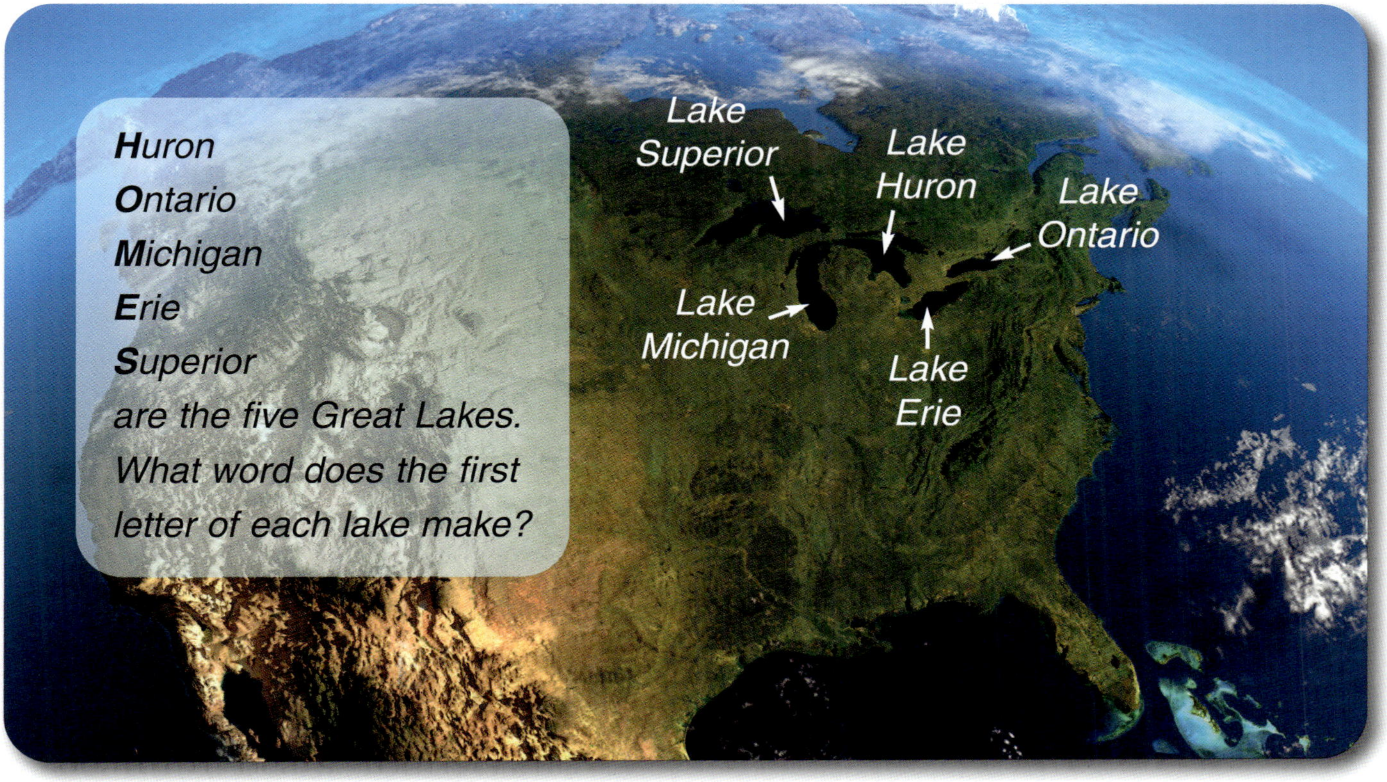

***H**uron*
***O**ntario*
***M**ichigan*
***E**rie*
***S**uperior*
are the five Great Lakes.
What word does the first letter of each lake make?

Lake Baikal, in Russia, is the oldest lake.
It has the most water, too.
Its water is deep and clean and pure,
and its color is clear blue.

Small lakes called ponds

Ponds are small, still, shallow lakes that are home to fish, frogs, birds, and snakes. Water lilies, hyacinths, cattails, and **sedges** grow in ponds and along their edges. Birds hide their nests among the weeds. Some line their nests with cattail seeds.

cattails

*This swan made a nest of leaves and sticks for her **cygnets**, or baby chicks.*

water hyacinth

sedge

Turtles **bask**
on rocks or logs.
They live in ponds
along with frogs.
Female frogs lay
clumps of eggs.
A tadpole hatches
with a tail, not legs.
The tail is replaced
as the froglet grows
by four strong legs
and eighteen toes.

This turtle is basking in the hot sun.
It will swim in the pond when it is done.

Rivers flow

Rivers flow from high ground to low.
They carry fresh water as they go.
The **source** of a river is where it begins.
The **mouth** of a river is where it ends.
Rivers **meander** in curves and bends.
They rush through rapids,
crash over rocks,
drop in waterfalls,
and make no stops,
until they reach a lake or a sea.
Can you find this river's mouth for me?

A small narrow river is called a **stream**. How shallow or deep does this water seem?

Many rivers from high mountains flow,
crashing powerfully over rocks below.
A river's path makes turns and bends
on the way to its mouth, where it finally ends.

Water everywhere

Most of Earth is covered in water.
Most of our bodies are water, too.
Our bones and brains
and the blood in our veins
need water to do the work that they do.
Without water, we could not survive!
Without water, we would not be alive.
Our hearts could not beat.
We'd be unable to eat.
Our brains could not think
without water to drink.

Plants and animals need water, too. They need water, just as we do.

Above and below

Water is in the clouds above
and in the ocean below.
It is what icebergs are made of
as well as the cold, white snow.
Water **evaporates**, melts, and freezes.
It blows in strong winds and gentle breezes.

The ocean is filled with fish to eat.
These penguins love a fresh fish treat!

Match them up!

The clues in the list
match the pictures you see.
Can you say what the matches might be?
Can you write your own rap
about how water helps you
and how you save water
and help keep it clean, too?
What are some things that you can do?

1. Which body of water is formed at low tide?
2. Which body of water is deep, huge, and wide?
3. In which water body does this boy have his hand?
4. Which big water body is surrounded by land?
5. Which one is hot, as you can see?
6. Which starts on a mountain and ends at the sea?
7. What can a small, shallow lake be?

Answers

1–E tide pool
2–D ocean (sea)
3–B lagoon
4–G lake
5–A hot spring
6–F river
7–C pond

Glossary

Note: Some boldfaced words are defined where they appear in the book.

bask To warm in the sun

clump A bunch of eggs that are close together

current A part of ocean water that is moving in a certain direction

evaporate To change liquid water into a vapor or mist

fresh water Water that does not contain salt

high tide A state of the ocean tide when it is at its highest level

hot spring Water that is heated naturally from the earth

low tide A state of the ocean tide when it is at its lowest level

midnight The zone of an ocean that is very deep, dark, and cold

recede To move away from shore

secluded Hidden away

shore The land along the edge of a lake, sea, or ocean

tide The alternate rising and falling of the ocean

tide pool A pool of water between rocks that is left at low tide

zone A section of an ocean

Index